5 BIBLICAL KEYS
TO UNLOCKING
WEALTH

BY
MARKITA BROOKS

FIRST EDITION

ISBN 978-1-7322243-0-8
Business & Economics . Christian Life: Professional Growth
Christian Life: Personal Growth

CREDITS

Cover design and layout by Kennesha M. Walker of Miwa Design and Graphics.

COPYRIGHT

All Scriptures are taken from the New King James Version of the Bible, unless otherwise noted. Scripture taken from the New King James Version®. Copyright © 1982 by Thomas Nelson. Used by permission. All rights reserved.

Scripture quotations marked "NIV" are taken from the Holy Bible, New International Version®, NIV®. Copyright © 1973, 1978, 1984, 2011 by Biblica, Inc.™ Used by permission of Zondervan. All rights reserved worldwide. www.zondervan.com The "NIV" and "New International Version" are trademarks registered in the United States Patent and Trademark Office by Biblica, Inc.™

Scripture quotations marked "CJB" are taken from the Complete Jewish Bible, copyright © 1998 by David H. Stern. Published by Jewish New Testament Publications, Inc., P.O. Box 615, Clarksville, Maryland 21029. www.messianicjewish.net/jntp. Used by permission.

LEGAL DISCLAIMER

This book, and none of its contents, should be taken as financial advice. Please contact a financial professional for specific advice regarding your situation or business (as advised in Key Three). Instead, receive this as it is, Biblical counsel for guiding your decisions when starting or growing a business or any other enterprise. For additional spiritual advice, seek an ordained spiritual leader such as myself, to make the best decisions possible in your life or business.—Markita Brooks, Kingdom Wealth, LLC

"Plans are established by seeking advice; so if you wage war, obtain guidance." —Proverbs 20:18
"Surely you need guidance to wage war, and victory is won through many advisers." —Proverbs 24:6

DEDICATION

This book is dedicated to:
My husband, my parents, my spiritual leaders
and every coach, mentor and trainer that has poured into me.
Thank You!

I especially want to dedicate this book
to my children and grandchildren.
May God continue to bless me,
so that I can leave a legacy and inheritance for you!

ABOUT THE AUTHOR

Markita Brooks is a wife, mother and grandmother, and she has been an entrepreneur since 2001. As Founder and CEO, she developed Kingdom Wealth, LLC, a company dedicated to creating wealth to do the most good. Through Kingdom Wealth, she serves as a writer, speaker and business coach to help others establish profitable businesses, so they can make a positive difference in the world. For 12 years, she was the president of a multiple 6-figure corporation. She has served as a business consultant for various enterprises and currently serves on the boards of directors for 5 non-profit organizations.

Markita is also the Founder and Senior Apostle of The Truth In The Spirit, a ministry that unites the Body of Messiah globally. She currently conducts business and religious trainings throughout the year, both live and online. As an author, her writings have been published in various magazines and periodicals, including self-publishing a book entitled, *The Road to Damascus: Transformation for the Next Level*.

Markita has a Bachelor's degree in Leadership Studies from the University of Richmond. She is a member of the International Who's Who of Professional Management, and has been featured in articles for professionals. Over the years, she has combined her spiritual insight and business experience to improve the lives of many around the world through writing, trainings, sermons, coaching and consulting. Connect with her to become successful in your own endeavors. Visit www.kingdomwealthllc.com to request her for a speaking engagement or to find out how you can connect with Kingdom Wealth, LLC to create wealth and do good in the world.

"I help current and potential business owners increase their income and make their businesses profitable, so they can make a positive difference in the world. I'm like a traveling locksmith providing keys on your journey to success!"

—MARKITA BROOKS
CEO OF KINGDOM WEALTH, LLC

TABLE OF CONTENTS

INTRODUCTIONS 1
In the Vineyard 2

KEY ONE: CONNECTION WITH GOD 4
Fellowship with God 8
Identity and Purpose 11

KEY TWO: SOUL PROSPERITY 14
The Makeup of Your Soul 15
Your Heart 15
Your Mind 16
Your Will 17
Soul Prosperity 18
Deliverance from Slavery and Oppression 19
Deliverance from Fear of Lack 22
Deliverance from Greed 24
Deliverance from Money-Loathing 25

KEY THREE: FINANCIAL STEWARDSHIP　　30
Start With What You Have　　31
Tithes, Offerings and Taxes　　32
Multiple Streams of Income and Investments　　34
Business Practices　　36
Accounting　　38
Debt　　42

KEY FOUR: PHYSICAL HEALTH　　46
Garbage In, Garbage Out　　47
The Temple of the Living God　　49
Rest　　50
Seeking God for Physical Healing　　51

KEY FIVE: INTIMATE RELATIONSHIPS　　54
Coaches, Trainers and Mentors　　55
Customers, Employees and Associates　　56
Family Relationships　　58
Intimacy with God　　59
More Opportunities　　60

5 BIBLICAL KEYS
TO UNLOCKING
WEALTH

INTRODUCTIONS

You and I are embarking on an amazing journey together. Though I'll be your guide, God Himself invited you. Let us begin with introductions. I am Markita Brooks—wife, mother, minister, entrepreneur—and I've heard the voice of God my entire life. Initially, I thought everyone could hear Him as I do. It wasn't until later in life that I came to understand that this was a special gift God had given me, so that He could speak into the hearts of people around the world. As we walk on this journey together, I know that God wants to speak into your heart. That's why He guided you to this book. He wants you to reach your full potential and become as successful as you ever dreamed, but that starts with prosperity in every area of life. That's what we'll explore together.

Though you may already be familiar with Him, the Lord would have me to introduce Him to you in a very specific way as well. Whether you feel you have an intimate relationship with God or not, He wants you to get to know Him better. As we journey through this book, He'd like you to see Him as an investor, a businessman and your Father. As such, He has created the most successful self-sustained, duplicable business system ever, and He has left it in the hands of His children. This business system is the earth, and He has given it as an inheritance to all of His children. You are a child of God. He made you in His image, endowed you with His creative ability and left a portion of the family business to you. You can do whatever you like with your inheritance, but it is your Father's will that you would develop your own talents, rightly steward the resources He has given you, and earn Him a return on His investment. As you journey through life seeking success, He wants you to remember that you can come to Him for guidance, strength and additional resources at any time.

Let us begin.

IN THE VINEYARD

In 2004, I had a vision. My clothing changed. I had on a sun hat and a long, gray, cotton dress with a white apron on the front of it. I thought I looked like a slave or servant, as the clothing seemed old-timey. I walked forward and approached the steps of a glorious mansion. The door was opened for me, and a man welcomed me in. Immediately, I knew He was the Messiah, the Son of God. I looked intently at Him, though my eyes could not perceive what I was seeing. The Son brought me down a hallway, with the intention of introducing me to the Father. I expected to be taken into a throne room or royal court, but the Father came down the hallway to meet us. As we approached the Father, the Son began to speak to Him. When I realized who He was, I immediately looked down, for fear that I might burst into flames or evaporate for looking at the Father. Then I heard the Son say, "She won't make it if she's not justified." The Father didn't speak, but I knew that He nodded His head in approval.

Then the Son took me out into the vineyard. The first section of the vineyard was well-tended, beautiful and flourishing. I said in my mind, *I'd like to have this section*, and I lingered there for a while. Then the Son beckoned me and said, "This is your section." He then drew me into a section of the vineyard that was overgrown, and some of the branches were dying. It was a mess. He said to me, "I need you to tend this section for me." It had clearly been neglected by others before me, but it must have held some importance to Him, so I humbly accepted the assignment. That's when I realized that I was dressed as a gardener. Then the vision ended.

God has a plan for the lives of each of His children. As we decide to walk with Him, He reveals more and more of that plan. If we decide not to walk in fellowship with Him, He'll allow us the freedom to walk where, how and with whomever we choose, but we will most likely squander the inheritance

He has given us. Yet, our choice to walk out this life with Him will always result in our individual destiny being fulfilled and great good being accomplished throughout the world. As our Father, He gives us an inheritance that corresponds with the gifts with which He has endowed us. Hence, we are uniquely and perfectly qualified to fulfill His plan for our lives. In fact, it is the only thing in which we will find satisfaction. The hard part is discovering God's will, while we are still discovering ourselves. This book is one of many invitations God is extending to you to partner with Him in this life, so that, together, you can do good in the lives of many. For you to accomplish this good, He must bless you with wealth.

- KEY ONE -
CONNECTION WITH GOD

*"Beloved, I **pray** that you may prosper in all things and be in health, just as your soul prospers."*

3 John 1:2

Everything we need for life, business and prosperity can be found in the Bible. It is God's owner's manual for your journey on earth. He would not give you a grand inheritance, an amazing destiny and unique gifts without also providing wise counsel for you. One Scripture in particular, 3 John 1:2, holds 5 Biblical Keys to Unlocking Wealth. We'll explore that Scripture, and many other supporting texts, to unlock wealth in your life, in five main areas, as they are all connected. Our focus as humans with limited understanding tends to lean toward financial resources, for fear that we will not have enough of them to accomplish our goals. However, I want to share with you that there are other areas of life that must be prosperous before you will experience financial prosperity. When you are prosperous in these areas, you will be successful in business and life, but when you are lacking in these areas, nothing you build will last. In this book, we will explore the 5 Biblical Keys together.

In the Scripture above, the words of Apostle John to his sons and daughters in the faith are actually a prayer to God. Prayer is the way we connect with God. As our Father and Creator, it's essential that we have a strong and personal connection with Him, which is the only way to truly know our own identity and purpose. I know who I am because of what God says about me. Because He created me, I believe Him. He's pretty much the foremost authority on me.

God created you, every fiber of your being. He placed you on earth within His perfect timing and with a plan in mind. You were designed in His image and given His creative ability. However, unlike everything else in creation, you were endowed with the power of choice. You can choose to come to Him to learn more about who you are and His plans for you, or you can decide to go it alone. You can lean upon His eternal wisdom or you can stumble about in the darkness. You can seek Him for the path He's laid out for you, or you can forge your own path. None of this changes His love for you. However, it will affect your success and fulfillment. As you truly get to know and appreciate yourself, you can build a creative enterprise around your gifts and abilities. That will always cause you to succeed, because you're providing unique products and services to the world.

In the beginning, God created the heavens and the earth (Genesis 1:1). It took Him six days to complete this process. Then He rested. Humankind was the last of His creation, yet we are the most important, because nothing else in creation was made in His image or given the authority to rule over the earth. When the man was created, he found himself in the Garden of Eden where everything he needed had already been provided (Gen. 2:8). Adam was born into abundant wealth. God desired to provide him a helper, so He pulled a rib from the man and created woman; then God presented the woman to the man and the two were one (Gen. 2:18-24). God blessed them to be fruitful and multiply and gave them dominion on the earth (Gen. 1:27-28). The man and woman had intimate fellowship with each other and God, and they felt no shame (Gen. 2:25).

This is how our lives were designed to be: intimate fellowship with God and each other, as we fulfill our purpose on earth. That purpose is fulfilled through your creative enterprises. However, the man and woman chose to disobey the one commandment God had given them—to abstain from eating the fruit from the Tree of the Knowledge of Good and Evil (Gen. 2:16-17)—and their lives changed forever. The enemy of their souls deceived them into disobeying God, and they experienced the consequences of that disobedience: striving, pain and death (Gen. ch. 3). In His great mercy, however, God sent His Son to atone for all of the sins of the world, so that humankind would no longer be bound in sin or afflicted with striving, pain and death (John 3:16). Now, it's our choice to return to intimate fellowship with God for His blessings upon our endeavors, as it was in the Garden of Eden, or to continue to remain outside of the grace and blessings of God to strive toward goals we can't reach without Him.

As you set out to start a business, ministry, organization or movement, you have to face the same choice that was before Adam and Eve. Do you want to build your enterprise within the blessings of intimate fellowship with God, thus fulfilling your purpose on earth? The alternative is to stay outside of God's grace and blessings to forge your own path. Please note that you will not be alone regardless of what you choose. God will always love you and be there for you, and the enemy of your soul will always seek to deceive you and rob you of success. However, choosing to walk with God significantly decreases the enemy's influence in your life and business. Choosing to walk away from fellowship with God makes you an immediate target for the deceptions of the enemy. Most people who believe they are choosing their own way only find out near the end of their lives that they have been fooled and they have been used for destruction—in effect, they have been destroying their own families and sowing seeds of destruction into their customers. That is not God's will for your business.

These deceptions of the enemy that lead to destruction come in many forms, but he tends to focus primarily on God's character, your identity and your purpose. If the enemy can get you to believe lies about God's character, and you were made in God's image, then he has an open door to begin to tell you who you are. Anything the enemy tells you serves only the purpose of usurping your God-ordained authority and giving it to the enemy. As we look at the 1st Biblical Key to Unlocking Wealth—Connection with God—we will focus on the 3 things about which the enemy lies the most, so that you can experience God's truth. Once you know the truth, your soul will reject the lies of the enemy, and you will be on your way to the fullness of the blessings that God has for you.

FELLOWSHIP WITH GOD

Most people have an image of God that is totally inaccurate. We tend to see Him as a judge, an oppressor or an egomaniac. I've actually had people say that to me, that they believe God must be an egomaniac because He requires so much worship. Nothing could be farther from the truth. Every standard that God sets in our lives, every requirement that He makes as we relate to Him, every commandment that He has ever given serve only to help us to be the most successful people that we can be. He created an entire universe, and then set us in it, with dominion on the only habitable planet. God designed everything with us in mind. He gave us unique talents and abilities and set us in a realm in which we can exercise the creative power and dominion with which He has blessed us. No parent can do better than that for their children. Our challenge then is to get to know Him, ourselves and our purpose, so that we can operate at maximum capacity and achieve ultimate success, which is fulfilling God's will for our lives through our enterprises.

God has many names, and each of them reveal an aspect of His nature and character. He revealed Himself to Abraham as God Almighty in Genesis 17:1. He revealed Himself to Hagar in Genesis 16:11-13 as the God who Sees. He revealed Himself to Moses in Exodus 3:14-15 as the great I AM, meaning He is everything we need Him to be. He is all encompassing. In Exodus 15:26, God reveals Himself as the God who Heals. He revealed Himself to Hannah as the Lord of the Hosts in 1 Samuel 1:11, because He leads the angel armies, fighting on our behalf. There are so many other names for God in the Bible, but you must get to know the many facets of His Presence for yourself. Each time you encounter Him, you'll get to know a little more about Him and yourself. You'll need your memory of these encounters as you go forward to fulfill your purpose on earth through your business.

Just as you would develop a relationship with anyone else, you must also develop a relationship with God. There are many ways to get to know God. You must create time and space for encounters with Him, so that your relationship can grow. The most notable difference between relating to God and relating to people, however, is that God is absolutely perfect. He never makes mistakes, He's completely trustworthy and He never fails. He is also your Father and Creator. So when you encounter challenges in your relationship with God, know automatically that He is right and true. Then, trust Him enough to show you the source of the challenge, so that together you two can address it.

In the time and space that you create for God, there are a few activities that are sure to engage Him. These include prayer, Bible study, worship and fasting. Prayer is merely a conversation with God. Bible study is an intimate time of reading and reflecting on God's Word, with the guidance of His Holy Spirit. Hence, you should pray first and ask God to guide your Bible study, so that you will understand and retain what you're reading. You also need God's Spirit to help you apply what you're reading to your daily life. Worship is using your words or another form of creative expression to convey the character and works of God. Yes, He knows who He is and what He has done, but your worship shifts your focus from your limitations and the challenges in this world to God's unlimited ability and unconditional love for you. Ultimately, worship serves the purpose of reminding your soul to focus on God. And He inhabits your praise, so it's like inviting Him into the room or situation. Lastly, fasting is a wonderful way to increase self-control and release control over to God. When you abstain from entertainment, food and beverages, you are choosing to turn your attention to God and away from comforts, which can dull you to God's will.

I spend the first 2 hours of each day with God in prayer, Bible Study and worship. I connect with God first before the rest of the world gets a chance to tell me what I should think and how

I should feel. All day long, we are bombarded with messages and suggestions. If we've not received God's Truth into ourselves first, we're open to all types of influences, even subconscious ones. I also live a lifestyle of fasting, which means that on any given day I deliberately abstain from at least one thing that makes me comfortable in order to insure that I hear clearly from God and develop a greater level of self-control, which is absolutely necessary to lead in the business world.

Now in addressing connecting with God, we must discuss sin. Sin is anything that is not God's will for our lives. Many sins are listed in the Bible, but there are things that God knows are harmful to us as individuals, which may not be listed in the Bible, so He reveals those things to us by His Spirit. Every person on earth sins, and every sin separates us from God. Sin puts a chasm between us, so that fellowship is strained. Sin is the pink elephant in the room when we want to connect with God. But God Himself gave us the remedy for that separation: He sent His Son to die for our sins. Our Messiah came to earth as a sacrificial lamb, to pay the price for every sin humanity will ever commit. The challenge for us is that we must believe that God loved us enough to do that, receive the price paid for our sins, and apply the cleansing Blood of Messiah to every sinful and broken area of our lives. He said that He came that we might have life and life more abundantly (John 10:10). If you've never accepted the Son of God as your personal Savior, pray and receive Him now. He's waiting on you.

As you establish your business, or seek to take it to the next level, let me encourage you to spend focused daily time connecting with God through prayer, Bible study, worship and fasting. In that time, God will heal your soul (which we'll get to in Key Two), reveal His will for your life and business and guide your decisions to reflect His perfect character. This will order your day and set you on a path to success. It will also fill you with hope, confidence and peace as you approach the challenges of the day. This is actually a practice of many of the wealthiest people in the world, because they have found it to be essential to their success.

IDENTITY AND PURPOSE

"Then God said, 'Let Us make man in Our image, according to Our likeness; let them have dominion over the fish of the sea, over the birds of the air, and over the cattle, over all the earth and over every creeping thing that creeps on the earth.' So God created man in His own image; in the image of God He created him; male and female He created them. Then God blessed them, and God said to them, 'Be fruitful and multiply; fill the earth and subdue it; have dominion over the fish of the sea, over the birds of the air, and over every living thing that moves on the earth.'—Genesis 1:26-28

Most people don't really understand the kind of relationship that God wants to have with us. This is because we tend to relate God to people in our lives, and those people are flawed, on their best days. God, on the other hand, is absolutely perfect and His love endures forever. He gave us choice so that we would have power. He wants to guide our choices, so that we will have success. Power without success is destructive failure. However, if we focus the personal power God gave us toward a clear vision, we will be creatively successful. I don't just mean we will have unique success. I mean our success will lead to innovation and hope for everyone and everything around us. Our creative success brings life and causes other things to regenerate or flourish, because God's creative force is at work in us.

Each of us has been blessed to be fruitful and multiply. The question that we must ask God is, "What type of fruit should I bear?" There is a purpose for which God designed you on earth. Your purpose will be linked to your interests, talents and abilities, but it will be completely focused on filling a need or solving a problem. When your interests, talents and abilities intersect to solve a problem or fill a need in the lives of others, you've found your purpose. This makes self-discovery in God's presence essential, because you will never discover your purpose until you know who you are, and who you are is only found in Him. He made you fearfully and wonderfully (Ps. 139:14), yet all you are is only revealed in the Light of His Presence.

The busyness of this world is designed to distract you from God's beauty and your uniqueness. The enemy would prefer that you never discover God's love or your purpose, because this allows wickedness to thrive unopposed on earth. You are God's secret weapon against pain, suffering and confusion. Through you He wants to bring clarity, healing and hope. But He can only use you, as He designed you, not the person you made yourself into in order to survive or to please others. He can't even use the person other people want you to be or the person the enemy has scared you into becoming. God needs the REAL YOU to step forward. For your true self to be revealed, He must address your soul.

- KEY TWO -
SOUL PROSPERITY

*"Beloved, I pray that you may prosper in all things and be in health, **just as your soul prospers.**"*

3 John 1:2

THE MAKEUP OF YOUR SOUL

Our souls consist of three parts: our thoughts, our emotions and our will. Most people associate thoughts with the mind, emotions with the heart and the will with our gut. Though these are physical body parts, and the soul is metaphysical, that association helps us to conceptualize something that is really beyond logic. Our souls are not physically tangible, yet they are the parts of us that will exist forever, so they are actually more real than our bodies. If you believe something in your mind and associate strong emotions with it, the choices that flow from your will are apt to generate a reality that is consistent with that which was in your soul. In short, our souls cause us to create our own realities. Is it really so hard to believe? God created the entire universe with His Words.

> *"Then God said, 'Let there be light'; and there was light."—Genesis 1:3.*

Similarly, our words flow from that which is in our hearts, and our words have the power of life and death. We will have what we say, and what we say will shape our environment or situation.

> *"For out of the abundance of the heart the mouth speaks."—Matthew 12:34b*

> *"Death and life are in the power of the tongue, And those who love it will eat its fruit."—Proverbs 18:21*

YOUR HEART

> *"Above everything else, guard your heart; for it is the source of life's consequences."—Proverbs 4:23 CJB*

So let us start with the heart. You have to guard it, because if it is damaged, it will harden to protect itself, and a hardened heart is cold, unfeeling and distant, even toward God. Now the truth is that you don't know how to guard your heart properly, because you didn't design it. As humans, we really don't know how fragile our emotions are. If we did, we'd be kinder and more gracious to ourselves and each other. God knows our hearts, so He teaches us how to guard them in His Word. This is another important reason to commit to daily Bible study and prayer. He also tells us that our hearts are deceptive in Jeremiah 17:9, which means my traumatized emotions can actually fool me into believing things that are not true and choosing destructive options for myself and my business, which I will pass on to my customers.

God, on the other hand, is a healer of hearts. He is able to isolate the trauma and extract all negative deposits into our hearts from traumatic experiences. Yet, He will only begin this work if we are willing to share our true feelings with Him. He's a Master Surgeon, and His first question is "Show Me where it hurts." That emotional pain, just like physical pain, is a sign of trauma. The earlier we share our "symptoms" with God, the faster our healing occurs. However, if we neglect wounds in our hearts for long, they can fester into a poison throughout our entire souls, reaching the thoughts and will as well. God can still heal us in these places, but there will be much more transformation required throughout our healing process, as the damage will have reached many areas, to include possibly our life choices, relationships and businesses.

YOUR MIND

"In other words, do not let yourselves be conformed to the standards of the 'olam hazeh [this present age]. Instead, keep letting yourselves be transformed by the renewing of your minds; so that you will know what God wants and will agree that what he wants is good,

satisfying and able to succeed."—Romans 12:2 CJB

Each of us has ways of viewing ourselves, the world and God. Our individual perspectives affect every decision that we make. If our thinking is flawed, our decisions will not be as effective at reaching our goals. If our perspective is skewed, we will absolutely miss our destination. For our thinking to be this important, it's no wonder advertisers, manipulators and the enemy of our souls work overtime to influence our thinking. Instead of being wrongly influenced, we need to bring our minds to God for renewal. We literally have to dump all of the garbage that has collected in our minds, so that there will be space in them for God's truths. It's not so much that we have limited memory capacity, but more importantly, competing information cannot survive in our minds. We are designed to be single in our focus, so clashing ideas will eventually have it out and one will win over the other.

YOUR WILL

"Let your eyes look straight ahead, fix your gaze on what lies in front of you. Level the path for your feet, let all your ways be properly prepared; then deviate neither right nor left; and keep your foot far from evil."
—Proverbs 4:25-27

Our will—personal preference based on our priorities—determines our choices. At the end of the day, we really only do what we want to do. That's why we have to let God address our emotions and thoughts first. As He heals our emotions, we can choose mature reactions to our situations. When our minds are renewed in an area, we will have a healthy, well-rounded perspective on things in that area. Our choices, which flow out of our will in the situation, will then be healthy for ourselves and others. This is essential if we truly want our businesses to do good in the earth. Selfish ambition and greed are easy, in the short-term. It's much harder initially to allow God to heal and cleanse us regularly, so that we will consistently make the tough choices that will produce the greatest good for everyone involved, ourselves included. For example, you may have to delay a large profit in order to legally and properly establish a division of your company. Each day we will be presented with decisions that will reflect our true priorities, ethics and morals. Allowing God to minister to our souls makes those decisions a non-question.

SOUL PROSPERITY

"Give, and you will receive gifts—the full measure, compacted, shaken together and overflowing, will be put right in your lap. For the measure with which you measure out will be used to measure back to you!"
—Luke 6:38 CJB

It is not enough for us to have healed souls. God wants to take us beyond that to prosperous souls. Prosperity is defined as a successful, flourishing, or thriving condition, especially in financial respects. For our souls to be prosperous, our minds must be continually filled with thoughts of success, our hearts must thrive on positive emotions and our wills must constantly produce wise and healthy choices that bring great returns for ourselves and others. That's a prosperous soul, and that is God's will for you. Additionally, it is absolutely necessary to build a profitable business that will do good for many people. Our God is a great investor, and all that He does for us is in hopes that it will spill over into blessings for others. He loves all of His children. As you get closer in relationship with Him, He will prosper you all the more, so that He can bless many others through you and your business. However, only a prosperous soul can handle those types of blessings.

The enemy of our souls has been working since our birth to lock us into bondage that causes us to malfunction. In order to truly have soul prosperity, we must be delivered from bondage in our souls. There are many different types of bondage for our souls, but we will focus on four that deal directly with money for now. As we spend more time together on this journey through Discovering Your Divine Design™ or Kingdom Business Masterminds™, I'll share more types of bondage that can negatively affect your business success, and we will address them together.

DELIVERANCE FROM SLAVERY AND OPPRESSION

Most of us have not actually spent years of our lives under a political system of slavery, but because slavery has been prevalent in human history, the enemy of our souls still uses it to put human souls into bondage. Because the enemy of our souls is a spirit not a human, I will call this spiritual bondage. The effects of spiritual bondage are the same as those of physical bondage. Slaves and the oppressed are stripped of their identities and power to make them dependent upon the oppressor. This ensures that they will be slaves forever, because every aspect of their lives, including their identities, becomes dependent upon the abusive relationship with the one enslaving them. The slave master, who in this case is the devil, enslaves for one reason: to usurp the personal power of those enslaved. This insures that his will is done and multiplied by the number of souls he is able to enslave with this spiritual bondage.

From birth to death, the enemy of our souls uses humans to try to make us feel unworthy, helpless and useless. These people are in spiritual bondage themselves, being used by the enemy to make slaves out of others. Once people began to believe these lies, demons are then assigned to continue to speak these negative suggestions into their souls, until the people start to believe that the suggestions of the enemy are their own thoughts. This is how he enslaves people's minds.

Individuals who think that they have no identity or purpose apart from unhealthy and demeaning relationships will never believe that God truly loves them. So, they then become estranged from the only One who can deliver them. Those attacks on their identities also bleed into pessimistic thoughts about life and humankind. Hence, people in spiritual bondage of slavery and oppression are always waiting for the other shoe to drop, believing that nothing can ever improve in their situation. The demons assigned in these cases actually sabotage opportunities and relationships to insure that situations never improve as well.

Similarly, negative thoughts lead to unhealthy emotions. We've already discussed that unhealed soul wounds can become like a cancer in the lives and businesses of those afflicted by them. The only healer is God, but this spiritual bondage instills such doubt, that its victims never reach out to God for healing. Hence, every pain, every attack, every form of abuse leaves a wound in the hearts of those spiritually enslaved and they are never healed. Their own hearts then become hardened and calloused, shutting out anyone who may actually love and care for them, thus locking them into a sort of "solitary confinement" in their own hearts. If people in this form of bondage ever establish a profitable business, they will pass on the spiritual bondage to their customers by selling destructive products and services.

A person in spiritual slavery may try to make choices that would improve on his/her life, but those choices will flow out of doubt and pessimism in the mind and unhealed wounds in the heart. Hence, this person will be incapable of receiving counsel or correction, because all of it will be perceived as another attack on their souls. Even constructive criticism will be viewed as a personal attack, rather than suggestions for improvement. Any idea that a person in spiritual slavery will have that is not positively received by everyone else in their lives will be then retracted and tucked back away in their hearts to hide it from further criticism. Hence, spiritual slavery then alienates people from those who could coach, mentor, teach and guide them—thrusting them back into dependence on their slave master. When people in spiritual bondage are in positions of leadership, they oppress all creative and honest people around them, choosing only to promote those individuals who agree with everything they say.

It becomes clear here why some people stay stuck in dead-end jobs and menial tasks their whole lives, or quickly rise to the top, only to plummet hard when their destructive practices are revealed. Their own thoughts, emotions and choices sabotage their success, and they become convinced that their lives can never improve and everyone is against them. Others may experience some level of success, but never fully reach their true potential, especially in doing good in the lives of those around them.

The only remedy for this type of bondage is to first recognize it for what it is: spiritual slavery and oppression. Then, you must acknowledge that the enemy is behind it, not the people and institutions he has used. Hence, all of the people and groups of people that were used by the enemy to cause you pain must be forgiven and released from debt (Matthew 6:12). Then you must realize that God has been waiting patiently all along to heal you.

If you desire to be free from spiritual slavery and bondage, you must confess all pain, woundedness, disappointments and offenses to God, and ask God to heal you. This may not be a quick process, because God has to address a lifetime of pain, but it is absolutely necessary. Then God's love must be allowed to flow into all of those areas that were wounded (through prayer, Bible study and worship), and the Blood of Messiah must be applied to each wounded area, for by His wounds we are healed (Isaiah 53:5). As the pain heals, true forgiveness will manifest in your heart as well. Then you will be empowered to bless people with your gifts and abilities, instead of causing greater destruction.

DELIVERANCE FROM FEAR OF LACK

Fear of lack is another form of spiritual bondage that manifests in people who have experienced extreme poverty or have been delivered from spiritual slavery. Those coming out of spiritual slavery were dependent upon whatever was oppressing them (this could even be a job or system), so once they get free, they fear for their provision. Others who have grown up in poverty or an unstable home environment may fear lack because they have experienced times when their personal needs went unmet, due to the irresponsibility or oppression of others.

As a mindset, the fear of lack focuses on daily provisions. Hence, a person with a fear of lack will be short-sighted. In their fear of not having something they will need in the future, they will waste or misappropriate resources today. There is also no understanding of delayed gratification for the purpose of ensuring one's future, because they already feel denied of essential needs, so as soon as anything comes to meet a need, the resource is quickly gobbled up. Business owners with a fear of lack sabotage their businesses by using all of the resources immediately, rather than wisely investing back into the business. When slow seasons come around, the business runs out of funds and may be forced to close.

Emotionally, people with a fear of lack have deep holes in their hearts. Not only have they lacked material resources, but they have also lacked support, affirmation and encouragement, leaving them thirsty for any type of compliment. This causes a tremendous problem, because they will lack discernment to know when people are complimenting them genuinely or when they have an ulterior motive. Hence, people with a fear of lack tend to befriend or enter into business partnerships with charismatic swindlers who take them for everything they have. So, the Scripture is fulfilled in them that reads, "For whoever has will be given more, and they will have an abundance. Whoever does not have, even what they have will be taken from them."— Matthew 25:29. This Scripture is not revealing God's heart. It reveals the tactics of the enemy against people who have not yet learned to believe God for provision. The enemy places that fear there. Then he uses it to rob them.

With a mindset of fear and a heart that needs immediate gratification, people with a fear of lack refuse to take the necessary risks to change their lives and start the type of business that will really make them successful. Because of that intense fear that they will not have what they need, they pass up opportunities that give a great return after a calculated risk. The fear in their minds makes it impossible for them to rightly calculate risks, because all the while a bright "DANGER" sign is going off in their heads. Their hearts will begin to pound uncontrollably, sending them into anxiety if anything changes in their financial situation, and they will stay committed to a dying endeavor because their fear of change has immobilized them. This is how a fear of lack affects a person's will.

The only remedy for fear of lack is faith in God. Faith is like a muscle, in that it must be exercised to become strong. If you identify a fear of lack within yourself, confess it to God and ask Him to remove it. Then ask Messiah to cover your soul with His Blood for healing every heart wound of poverty or instability that first introduced this fear into you. As you began to walk out of fear and into faith, meditate on Matthew chapter 6 regularly for God to begin to renew your mind, and take steps each week to obey the Messiah's words in that chapter. Next, commit your finances to God, and begin to demonstrate that commitment in your financial management, starting with your tithe, which is the first 10% of your income (Malachi 3:6-12). As we get into the Financial Stewardship Key, be sure to put that wisdom into practice, while praying and fasting, so that God can guide and strengthen you. He knows you're coming out of fear, so His Spirit will guide you slowly, but challenge yourself to take baby steps of obedience, because this will lead to your freedom.

DELIVERANCE FROM GREED

The spiritual bondage of greed works very similarly to the other two except that a person must have an abundance of resources to truly develop greed. People in poverty who appear to be greedy are actually suffering from a fear of lack. If it goes unchecked and they do acquire abundant wealth, it can quickly turn to greed, however. Spiritual bondage to greed comes from a lack of appreciation for God's provision. A greedy person fails to acknowledge that God is the One who has provided the wealth (Deut. 8:18), so they spend their wealth on selfish pursuits. Greedy people can be fooled into believing they are benevolent, by giving a portion of their income to charity. If charitable donations are given only to gain tax credits, then that still comes out of greed for selfish gain. The motives of a greedy person are always selfish at their core, so it becomes so important that our heart motivations are regularly tested by God.

In spiritual bondage to greed, the enemy convinces people that their personal identities are linked to their wealth. Hence, they would believe they were nothing without money and the luxuries it provides. Greedy people measure success by material wealth only and judge others by that measure. They also believe they are solely responsible for making the money, so they are quickly given to pride. The thoughts that pervade a greedy person's mind are thoughts of gain, selfish ambition and the pride of life (1 John 2:16).

The heart of a greedy person may not have been wounded in the past, but it will become wounded by the sin of greed and an insatiable lust for more. Eventually money will become an idol in the heart of a greedy person, causing them to see the bottom line as the deciding factor in all decisions and damage their relationships with God and everyone around them.

Matthew 6:19-24 reveals what happens in the heart of a greedy person. This text starts with a Hebrew idiom about a good and bad eye. A person with a good eye is generous, always looking for ways to help and give. A person with a bad eye is stingy, always looking for more that they can acquire. Eventually that "bad eye" will become covetous and desire even other people's money, possessions, spouses, etc.

The Lord reveals to us in this text that the stingy person with the "bad eye" is dark inside, like a star that burns out, turning into a black hole. Rather than producing warmth and light, a black hole sucks in everything around it, creating such great pressure that the items sucked in implode. Greed is that powerful in the hearts of humans, turning good people into selfish hoarders that serve the idol of Mammon rather than God. Mammon is the demonic force behind greed, so we must ask God to continually cleanse us of any greedy thoughts or heart motivations.

If you find yourself stuck in bondage to greed, confess that to God, and ask Messiah to cleanse and protect you with His healing Blood. Sacrificial giving (giving until it hurts) is a surefire way to complete the process of ridding yourself of greed. As with fear of lack, following the financial management prescriptions in the Financial Stewardship Key in this book will keep God's people out of the hands of Mammon and free from the bondage of greed.

DELIVERANCE FROM MONEY-LOATHING

This particular spiritual bondage, money-loathing, is the first form of financial bondage from which God delivered me. It tends to manifest itself in God's people because of a very specific demonic attack waged against us by the enemy.

*"For the **love of money** is a root of all kinds of evil. Some people, eager for money, have wandered from the faith and pierced themselves with many griefs."–1 Timothy 6:10 NIV*

Now this is an important truth. Paul was speaking of ministers who use the gospel for personal gain, rather than service to God and His people. The challenge here is that the enemy has twisted this Scripture in the minds of believers to think that money is the root of all evil. This is a lie dispatched for the purpose of keeping God's people impoverished so that we will never be able to do God's will. It also causes us to look down on ministers who receive pay for our work, and causes the families of ministers to resent God for failing to provide for His people. There are many more effects of it, like missions trips that we are not able to fund, assistance to the poor in our communities that we are unable to give, and losing the best talent within the Body of Messiah to high-paying secular jobs because people need to take care of their families.

This perversion of that Scripture causes believers to literally hate money, for fear that being prosperous will cause them to turn away from God. Nothing could be further from the truth. When God is trying to bless His people to do His work in the earth and we turn away from His provision, we are in fact turning away from Him and His will for our lives and ministries. Our God is a strategist and an investor. Whenever He calls us to a work, He also grants us provision for the work, but we have to begin to see money as another tool in our hands. This same lie keeps many believers from being prosperous business people. Instead of employing sound business practices, believers tend to mismanage their finances and call it faith. Money is neither evil nor good; money reflects the heart motivations of the person directing its use. This makes it all the more important that we commit our mindsets, heart motivations, wills and finances to God. He is well able to direct our use of finances, without allowing prosperity to lead us to greed.

Bondage to money-loathing is hard to detect because it is subconscious in most people. Many of us would agree that money is neither good nor evil, but in the minds of those who loathe it, it is the source of evil. I remember whenever I would get money into my hands, I would want to get rid of it as soon as I could. I'd bless someone or buy something for someone else, all to insure that I was not being overcome with greed. However, there was never anything greedy in me. Instead, there was a fear that money would defile me. I had seen people waste money, become obsessed with money, and actually give up their most important relationships in life for money, and I wanted no parts of that. As far as I was concerned, money could make people evil. I did not understand that it was the enemy at work in those people I had encountered, but he was also at work making me hate money.

God has always made it clear that He would bless me. I received a prophecy that everything I touched would prosper, and indeed I have witnessed that in my life, unless there's a demonic attack against me of which I am unaware. In this case of money-loathing, the enemy ensured that I would not be prosperous in that season of my life by convincing me that I had to get money as far away from me as possible. Thank God for opening my eyes to this deception and teaching me to welcome His blessings!

I am certainly not the only believer who has needed to have their mind renewed in this area. I have watched believers give away or spend thousands of dollars in a few weeks, then be destitute the next week. This is not God's will. Every dollar, every penny, God gives us serves a purpose. He either wants us to sow it into His Kingdom, bless someone in His Name, invest in a business venture (to grow our money), save it for a future need or use it to meet current needs. If we use our money in a way that it is not intended to be used, we will have a deficit in the future. We've got to get to the place in which we seek God regularly for His direction in our financial management. He gives us provision for a specific vision. At any given time, we need to know God's vision for the provision.

People who suffer from spiritual bondage to money-loathing are also afraid. However, they are not afraid of lack. They are afraid of displeasing God, but this is the wrong type of fear. Proverbs 1:7 tells us that the fear of God is the beginning of wisdom. However, it does not mean "terror"; it means "reverence". Reverence is a deep, respectful love of something or someone that is held in high esteem. When the Bible speaks of the fear of God, it means to take Him, His ways and His commandments seriously, to put Him first in all things. It does not mean that we should be terrified of displeasing Him. This terror will cause us to fear making mistakes, which is an important part of our relationship with God and success in business. God gently corrects our mistakes. He doesn't cast us out of His Presence for eternity because of them. In fact, He has already provided the remedy for consequences of our mistakes, by sending His Son to die for us. This does not mean that we should commit willful sins, but it does allow us grace to come to God to help us address our errors.

People in spiritual bondage to money-loathing may also fear the effects of greed. Like me, they may have seen greed turn good people into monsters, and they've developed a fear that it could happen to them. Here is yet another opportunity to trust God. He is able to protect His people from the attacks of the enemy and keep our souls safe from harm and defilement.

Once I acknowledged that I had been deceived into this form of bondage, God had to renew my mind about prosperity. The enemy had actually convinced me that poverty made me even more righteous. If money has no intrinsic value, then poverty has no ability to sanctify. Sacrifice is an important part of our walk with God, but He trains us to sacrifice much better with finances than without. When we're prosperous, God can cause us to give even more, requiring greater sacrifice, which will improve our character. However, He can also choose to allow us to only have basic needs met during other phases of life, so that we will learn to abase and abound, to be in need and have plenty, as Paul did (Phil. 4:12). All of this leads to wisdom and good financial stewardship, which is necessary for God's people to learn, as we prepare for His will to manifest in our lives through our businesses.

To be fully delivered from bondage to money-loathing, we must renounce a hatred for money and welcome God's blessings, in every form, but especially in finances. As a part of the mind renewal, believers coming out of this bondage need to spend lots of time reading about God's people who were blessed to be prosperous like Abraham in Genesis chapters 12-25, Isaac in Genesis chapters 25-26, Jacob in Genesis chapters 25-36, Joseph in Genesis chapters 37-50, David in 1st & 2nd Samuel, 1st Chronicles and many of the Psalms, Solomon in 1st Kings chapters 1-11, Ecclesiastes and Proverbs, as well as the women who provided for the Lord's ministry in Luke 8:1-3. There are many others whom God blessed with prosperity, and our Messiah gives more parables about financial wealth than anything else. Our finances are important to God, just like every other area of life. We must submit our thoughts and emotions about money to our Father, so that He can transform our thinking and heal our hearts, to make room for His prosperity.

- KEY THREE -
FINANCIAL STEWARDSHIP

*"Beloved, I pray that you may **prosper in all things** and be in health, just as your soul prospers."*

3 John 1:2

The Bible focuses on financial stewardship a lot. In fact, as I mentioned earlier, our Messiah gave more parables about finances than about anything else. Our financial resources are important to God. He is the One who has given us the power to create wealth (Deut. 8:18), so we must honor Him with our finances. Understanding that all of our financial resources come from God and allowing God to direct our use and management of those finances is good financial stewardship. Just as with any wise investor, God will give more to those who have proven themselves to be faithful stewards, and those who are unfaithful stewards will continually be robbed by the enemy until they have nothing left.

> **"For anyone who has something will be given more, so that he will have plenty; but from anyone who has nothing, even what he does have will be taken away."**
> **—Matthew 13:12 CJB**

START WITH WHAT YOU HAVE

When God's people gain an understanding of His will to bless us with financial wealth, we often don't know where to start. It takes money to make money, as investing and starting a business both require finances. Unless we grew up among entrepreneurs and investors, we tend to think that we have nothing to work with. However, God always asks us, "What do you have?" and commands us to start there. When He called Moses to lead the Israelites out of Egypt, God asked Him, "What is that in your hand?" It was a staff, and God blessed that staff to perform miracles (Ex. 4:1-5). When the indebted widow asked the prophet Elisha to help her to save her children from slavery, he asked her, "What do you have in your house?" She replied that there was only a little bit of oil, and he blessed the oil to multiply. She had to borrow jars to catch it all. Then she sold the oil to pay her debt (2 Kings 4:1-7). When the disciples asked the Lord how they were to feed the multitudes that had come to hear Him speak, He asked them, "How many loaves do you have?" Then He multiplied the loaves and fed thousands (Mat. 15:32-38). When we want to start a new financial endeavor, God's question of us is always the same, "What do you have?"

God doesn't ask us this question because He doesn't know. He asks to inspire us to take an inventory. We always have more than we think we do. He has given all of us the power to create wealth, so there are multiple seeds in your life now that you can sow to reap a return. Ask God to help you identify what you have that you can invest in your business and yourself. He is capable of opening your eyes to that which He has already given you.

You will note that all of our examples included individuals working in a community as well. Shortly after God anoints Moses' staff, He sends his brother Aaron to help him speak to the people and to Pharaoh. Elisha tells the widow to borrow clay jars for the olive oil from her neighbors. The Lord asks all of his disciples how many loaves they have. Among the 12 of them, they could only round up a few. However, this is important because God is teaching us not only to count the financial resources we have within our direct household, but He also wants us to count the resources with which we have access through our relationships. This is a key factor in building wealth, which is why the 5th Biblical Key is Intimate Relationships. God will always connect us with people and institutions around us to help us create more wealth. So, start releasing independence and pride to Him right now, as many of your blessings will come through people around you.

TITHES, OFFERINGS AND TAXES

"Then he said to them, 'So give back to Caesar what is Caesar's, and to God what is God's.'"
—Matthew 22:21b NIV

Good financial habits are best created before you receive serious income. That's because it's much easier to manage a small amount of money than it is to manage larger sums. Our tithes, offerings and taxes should be based upon a percentage of our gross income (income before expenses), so that they will all increase as our income increases.

God requires 10% of everything we earn. This is called a tithe, which means "tenth" (Matt. 23:23). This is not negotiable, as He states that the first 10% is already His (Lev. 27:30-32). In fact, it is a test of our stewardship. If we are willing to give Him what is already His, we will willingly allow Him to direct the use and management of the 90% that is ours as well. Our offerings, which are freewill gifts to God, come out of the 90%, and we determine the amount (Mal. 3:6-12). However, it should be a percentage of all gross income, so that it also increases as our income increases. To learn more about sowing tithes and offerings into God's Kingdom, speak with your spiritual leader, and if you don't have one with whom you can make personal contact, ask God to direct you to the spiritual leader of His choosing. He or she may be instrumental in helping you to establish and grow your business with God's blessings.

Taxes are owed to our federal, state and local government entities for communal expenses like roads and schools, as well as community and civic programs. As business owners, it is our responsibility to be sure that our taxes are calculated accurately and paid in a timely manner to the representative tax agencies on the local, state and federal levels. There are stiff penalties for failing to do so, and these penalties can cause businesses to close. As your business grows, it will be essential that you find an experienced and trustworthy accountant to handle your taxes and monitor your bookkeeping. Most established CPAs will take legal responsibility for errors on your business taxes as well. They may not, however, give you Biblically sound advice with regard to sowing from your business into the Kingdom of God.

This is why you should establish how much you will sow with your spiritual leader first. Then tell your CPA your plans, and ask him/her to help you do so within the confines of the tax laws.

MULTIPLE STREAMS OF INCOME AND INVESTMENTS

"Send your resources out over the seas; eventually you will reap a return. Divide your merchandise into seven or eight shares, since you don't know what disasters may come on the earth."—Ecclesiastes 11:1-2 CJB

Many people will encourage you to get into business and make moves quickly, especially if they will make money off of your choices. Yet only a few mentors and coaches will tell you what you need to consider before choosing to start a business and at every level of business development. I'll tell you that the most important thing you want to consider is whether or not your 3 most precious and limited resources can sustain the rigors and sacrifice of starting your own business or scaling your business. Can your energy level, your time and your finances sustain you through the development or growth of a business? Most businesses fail within the first five years because the business owners never asked themselves this question. I'd like you to pause now and answer this question honestly, in the Presence of God.

If you've concluded that you do have enough energy and time to start a business (or you'll sacrifice to "create" more of both), now you've got to take a good look at your financial situation. Your business will take time to actually turn a profit and become self-sustaining. During those years, you've got to be able to sustain your life, your family and your business on your own personal finances. Is that something you are willing and able to do? You should have multiple income sources now, and commit to continuing to work those until your business is successful. If you are unsure about how to create multiple streams of income, do some research. For additional guidance, plan now to be a part of my Prosperity Coaching™, because creating multiple streams of residual income is one of the first things I suggest. As you build your business, you also want to make sure your credit rating is good and you're decreasing your debts, because you may need to borrow money to grow your business. Yes, the borrower is slave to the lender (Prov. 22:7), but debt can be helpful if it provides needed resources within an established timeframe that will allow you to make significantly more income than you're ultimately losing in interest. This is one of those calculated risks we discussed earlier. As your business grows, your investments and savings will then provide needed cash flow in times of growth and development. In fact, you may then become the lender to many.

From the Scripture at the beginning of this section, we see that God advises us to have a diverse financial portfolio. This will include residual income from different sources, preferably in different industries, in case there are unforeseen challenges that affect an entire industry (like the banking crisis a few years ago). Investments should follow the same wisdom. As your business grows, and you earn money that you can afford to risk (meaning if you lose it all, your business will not fail), then you should begin to invest in various markets with varying levels of risk. Hence, your investment portfolio should include some low-risk and some high-risk investments, as well as investments in various markets. As the Scripture states, we don't know what will do well, so diversifying is the best way to insure a return on our investment. In most cases, some of our investments will do well, and others will not. A diverse portfolio protects against losing all of your investment at once. As with everything, enter into investments with prayer and wise counsel.

BUSINESS PRACTICES

When we view how often God addresses business practices in the Bible, we understand that it is almost assumed that God's people will be business owners. He has designed us to be creative, given us dominion over the earth's resources and blessed us to be fruitful and multiply. All of that is beautifully expressed in business ownership. As a business owner, you are taking responsibility for stewarding a portion of the earth's resources to meet needs in your community. That makes you a representative of God on earth. Should we choose to operate within His Kingdom Wealth Principles, we'll build hope and faith in others, while blessing them through our good stewardship. If we choose to ignore God's Kingdom Wealth Principles in our business practices, the enemy will capitalize on our rebellion by using us to rob and oppress those around us (Prov. 29:2).

God knew how important this would be, so He set Biblical standards for business practices. Genesis 2:15 reveals that God gave the man one responsibility: to tend the garden. We have been given access to many resources on earth. Your business is the section of God's vineyard that He is charging you with tending, just as He asked me to tend a portion of His vineyard in the vision at the beginning of this book. I help God's people to create wealth to do the most good. With what has He charged you? Take that stewardship seriously, as you are converting God's resources (to include intellectual property) into something useful in people's lives and businesses (Col. 3:23). Tend your portion of the vineyard so well that you produce much with little and bless many from your endeavors. That's innovation, and people will gladly pay for it, which will make your business profitable (Prov. 10:4).

Never concern yourself with making a quick buck. God's processes take time, because He is establishing a sure foundation for you. Instead, focus on building a business that will provide true value for people, turn a huge profit in the long-run and bring glory to God. Endeavors that promise to make quick cash for you or your business are not blessed by God (Prov. 12:11 & 20:21), and they will prove to cost more than they gain (Prov. 21:5). Instead, diligently work toward every goal you and God set together, and enlist the long-term support of others who are also invested in your vision. This will require patience from everyone involved, but don't be afraid to ask God for it (despite the religious rhetoric against praying for patience); it is a fruit of the Spirit (Gal. 5:22-23).

God has given you many abilities and talents, but you are responsible for training and developing them, in yourself and your staff. Invest lavishly in training and development, because it yields the greatest return. You will be blessed to be surrounded by capable people, and they will return your investment with loyalty and strong work ethics. They will believe in your vision, because they realize that you believe in them. Then ask God to anoint the gifts and talents you've invested in training (Ex. 35:30-35). God's anointing can empower you all to do exponentially more than you could imagine or dream.

Be sure to take good care of your employees, providing whatever benefits you can afford. And pay them well and promptly (Lev. 19:13). Settle their grievances with you and each other in ways that demonstrate God's standards for justice, as well as His compassion and grace (Job 31:13-14). This will bring God's blessings upon you, and insure that you attract and retain the top people in every skillset needed for your business to succeed. If you incur a loss, take the loss yourself (Gen. 31:39), without passing it onto your employees, if possible. God will honor your diligence and bless you when other businesses in your industry are losing badly (Gen. 26:1 & 26:12-13). As you continue in these Biblical business practices, be sure to remind the Lord in prayer, and ask for His blessing regularly (Neh. 5:19).

Be honest in all of your transactions and make integrity in business a standard among your employees (Deut. 25:13-15). Set fair prices and put your customers first, while your employees are watching. This will model the behavior and attitude you want to see in them. Reward those who demonstrate high morals and excellent customer service within your organization. Be careful when considering fostering competition and using incentives based solely on sales performance, as these tactics tend to communicate to staff that profits are more important than customers. As a business leader, you never want to consciously or unconsciously communicate that to your staff, because it will bear horrible fruit in the culture of your business and eventually in the profit margin.

Remember to be generous to yourself—the boss and business owner. Set yourself a salary that not only meets your personal financial needs, but also blesses you for your hard work (1 Tim. 5:18). Most people in the world don't have a problem with this one, but believers tend to struggle here, because we put everything and everyone before ourselves. Yes, Messiah calls us as leaders to be servants of all (Matt. 20:26). However, that does not mean that everything should be a sacrifice and we are never to reap the rewards of our own labor. When deciding upon your own salary (and you should review this at least annually), check your books to see what the business can comfortably afford to pay you, but then ask your trusted advisors for their input. In most cases, they will suggest that you pay yourself more than you were planning, because they see your worth and are in your life as agents of God to help you see it too.

ACCOUNTING

In Luke 16:1-13, Messiah shares a parable about a shrewd manager with His disciples. Like most things in Scripture, this parable has levels of meaning. For the purpose of this book, we'll look at what He is teaching us about accounting. This manager, or steward, is accused of wasting the wealth of his employer, a rich man. The wealth for which the rich man demands an account is his own wealth, not the wealth of the manager. The manager was merely supposed to help the rich man manage his finances. However, when the rich man asked the manager to give an account for the finances, the manager could not do so. Now let us look at this carefully. What this means practically is that the manager of the rich man's funds had kept no record of the funds coming in as income nor of the funds going out as expenses. Hence, he could not tell the rich man how much money he had currently or what was owed to him. The rich man then could not make any intelligent decisions about his own finances because nothing was known about the actual amounts he had coming in or going out.

So, when the manager realized he was going to be fired, he brought in all of the rich man's debtors. He asked each of them how much they owed his master. The manager should have been able to tell the debtors how much they owed, but because he was not keeping record of the finances, he had to ask them what they owed his master. Each one brought their bills in to prove what they owed. (The manager didn't even have copies of the bills he gave them.) The manager then had them change their bills, thereby forgiving some of their debts. Since he had kept no records, this would be the only way the rich man could get back any part of what was owed to him. So, the next day, the manager now had a record of what was owed to his master, even though the amounts were lower than they should have been. The rich man then congratulates the manager for creating a record quickly, when initially there was not one.

Now, the Lord gives us this parable not to encourage us to falsify records. His point is that the manager realized that he lost favor with his master, so he used his authority over the master's financial resources to gain favor with the master's debtors. The lesson to us is to use God's wisdom as we steward the wealth God has given us, realizing that good relationships with people are more important than profits in the long-run.

> ***"The master commended the dishonest manager because he had acted shrewdly. For the people of this world are more shrewd in dealing with their own kind than are the people of the light. I tell you, use worldly wealth to gain friends for yourselves, so that when it is gone, you will be welcomed into eternal dwellings. Whoever can be trusted with very little can also be trusted with much, and whoever is dishonest with very little will also be dishonest with much. So if you have not been trustworthy in handling worldly wealth, who will trust you with true riches? And if you have not been trustworthy with someone else's property, who will give you property of your own?"—Luke 16:8-12 NIV***

If we accept that all of our finances are a gift from God and we want to honor God in our finances, we will use Godly wisdom in managing those finances. God cares more about human souls being connected in right relationship with Him for all eternity than He does about material wealth that He can easily replace. As His children, we should value people higher than wealth, and allow God to direct the management of our resources to be a blessing to others. This is assuming that we have been delivered from money-loathing, our motivations come solely from a desire to please God and our actions are guided by His Spirit.

In order to be in a position to respond when God calls us to sow into the lives of others or into a major project in His Kingdom, we must have an accurate accounting of our personal and business finances. This will allow us to immediately assess whether or not we can afford to respond. Even if we decide to sow sacrificially (meaning we can't actually afford to do it without affecting a personal or business need), we still must know the amount to ask God to replace so that all needs will be met. This is essential in guiding us into effectual, fervent prayers (James 5:16). Our God answers specifically, and mature prayers must include specific amounts, which are made possible only through precise and up-to-date accounting.

Every business, no matter the size, must be sure that the three most important functions of accounting are met: bookkeeping, tax filing and financial accountability. As a business owner, you need not be responsible for the bookkeeping yourself. However, be sure to hire a bookkeeper who is significantly more responsible and honest than the manager in our analogy. The person keeping record of your finances will be one of the most important people in your operation, so choose wisely, stay close to them and set regular times to review the books for accountability. If challenges or errors arise in the bookkeeping, you want to be made aware of it as soon as possible, and regular in-house audits is the best way to do this.

Tax filing and payments are essential to any business. The size of your business will determine your frequency in payments, but you should always employ a Certified Public Accountant (CPA) to prepare your business taxes. Often times, they will assume responsibility for any errors on your tax forms. Get tax advice throughout the year, to insure that you're operating wisely all year. Otherwise, you'll be hit with unwelcome surprises at the time of annual filing.

If your business has become very successful financially, then an annual audit by an independent CPA (that is not your bookkeeper) will help you to find any issues in your bookkeeping. Do not rely on the transfer of information from your bookkeeper to your CPA to replace this annual audit, because the CPA will submit your tax returns based on the records provided by your bookkeeper. Only an independent audit will truly catch errors, theft and mismanagement. The more income coming in, the greater the opportunity for theft and mismanagement. Accounting is essential, so build professional habits as you scale your business.

Remember also that God and any investors, Board members (if you have a corporation) or potential business partners will want proof that you are able to manage the finances of your business well. In fact, certain licenses, loans and supporters will require the annual independent audit report that we just discussed. Why? The Lord makes it clear in His interpretation of the parable above: no one will trust you with more resources if you haven't been a good steward over those you already have at your disposal. This includes God. So take your accounting seriously, and allow your accounting processes to grow with your business. You won't need multiple CPAs when you're the only employee of your company, but be sure that all of the necessary functions of bookkeeping, tax preparation and financial accountability are being covered at your current prosperity level, and prepare for your accounting processes to change as your business grows.

DEBT

"If someone sues you, come to terms with him quickly, while you and he are on the way to court; or he may hand you over to the judge, and the judge to the officer of the court, and you may be thrown in jail!"
—Matthew 5:25 CJB

There are many Scriptures about debt, like the one above, and they all share God's wisdom concerning dealing with debt. The first advice God gives us is "don't" (Prov. 22:7)—don't get into debt at all. In a perfect society built completely upon God's Kingdom Wealth Principles, our grandparents would provide an inheritance for us (Prov. 13:22), so that when we wanted to start a business or buy a home, they would have enough money to give it to us or at least finance it initially for us. This would cause us to owe them only the principle amount of the loan (if anything at all) as we grow in wealth ourselves, because God forbids His people from charging interest on loans within His kingdom family (Ex. 22:25 & Deut. 23:20).

As the believers in our lives become financially prosperous, they model for us the truth about debt: we don't need it in order to thrive. We will need help, but prosperous friends and family members can take the place of loans and credit from financial institutions, bringing us all closer to the system of cooperative economics that God intended for His people.

We, however, do not live in an ideal society built on God's Kingdom Wealth Principles, so we often require loans and credit from financial institutions in order to initially fund the next level opportunities God puts before us. He is not caught unaware by this, so He tells us what to do if we must borrow money. The Scripture above reminds us to respect the relationship between lender and borrower. Since borrowing money makes us slaves of the lender (Prov. 22:7), it's essential that we honor the commitments we make, so that we will not be forced to suffer under the penalties to which we agreed.

Whenever we are unable to honor our repayment commitments as agreed, Messiah teaches us to settle the disputes immediately and personally, with some type of arrangements that we initiate, in order to keep ourselves from receiving the full extent of the punishment for breaking the agreement (Prov. 22:26-27). Most creditors (including the IRS) are willing to work with you if you communicate with them regularly. It actually costs them more money to prosecute you than to make a payment arrangement with you or even forgive a portion of your debt. If you find yourself in a financial bind and unable to fulfill your commitments to creditors, pray first, so that God can remove any fears that would cause you to ignore your responsibilities or make a rash decision, like taking the first arrangement they offer you if you really cannot fulfill it. Once God ministers to you, you will be filled with the confidence to honestly look at your finances and make arrangements with your creditors that you can actually handle.

As we discuss debt, it is also important that I share with you God's Kingdom Wealth Principle of paying back what we owe. Psalm 37:21 teaches us that only wicked people borrow and do not repay. This means that we are considered wicked financial stewards in God's eyes if we borrow money with no intention or effort to pay it back.

The second half of Proverbs 13:22 shares that the wealth of the wicked is stored up for the righteous. As God's people, we often like to believe that the financial institutions are wicked, and we are righteous victims of their greed when we have to repay money we borrowed from them. Biblically speaking, this is inaccurate. When we borrow money and don't repay it, we are acting wickedly in God's eyes, because we are untrustworthy with someone else's resources. That's why when we don't repay, they have the right to claim our possessions, because our wealth (as wicked people) is now going to the righteous lenders. That sent me reeling when I understood it. If you really want to be a righteous steward, ask God to provide the income for you to pay back all of your debts, with no charge-offs. That's hard, but it's the best way.

The Bible also teaches us that getting into debt on behalf of others (co-signing loans) is foolish (Prov. 6:1-5 & 17:18). If we want to bless someone, it is much better to give them money ourselves or grant them an interest-free loan from our own finances. This will allow us to be a blessing to them in resources, but it will also give us an opportunity to teach them to be good stewards. People are much more likely to listen to your advice if you have shown that you care by helping them. Then your advice will be received as wise counsel, rather than condemning judgment. Also, you can make them receiving this advice from you, and even some level of financial accountability to you, a requirement of them receiving the gift or loan. This is not pushy; it's good stewardship over the finances God has given you and it is a blessing to those you are helping, whether they realize it or not.

- KEY FOUR -
PHYSICAL HEALTH

*"Beloved, I pray that you may prosper in all things and **be in health**, just as your soul prospers."*

3 John 1:2

God has put a wealth of talents and gifts inside of you, but He did not stop there. He encased those gifts within a complex and finely-tuned machine that is capable of mass production and regeneration. That machine is your body. The human body is the most complex system in the universe, because it is filled with multiple complex systems: the nervous system, the digestive system, the reproductive system, the integumentary (skin) system, the respiratory system, the muscular system, the skeletal system and so much more. Science cannot fully comprehend or duplicate all that God has done in this complex and highly functioning machine that is worth billions of dollars, but God has given it to you as a free gift! All He requires is that you feed it, exercise it, clean it and take care of it.

As our Creator, He has also been kind enough to provide for us an owners' manual for our bodies called the Bible. In it, we learn what is healthy and what is not. We learn what will bless the body and what will destroy it. We learn what to put into and on our bodies and what we should abstain from. It is important that we demonstrate our appreciation to God by taking care of these priceless gifts. But it is also a benefit to us. The better we treat our bodies, the greater our ability to succeed at everything God puts before us, including our businesses. Our bodies are literally the vehicles that carry us to our success. You will find that everything in life, especially running a business, is much harder when you are physically unhealthy. It is our job to understand how durable, yet fragile, our bodies really are and take them back to our Creator when they malfunction.

GARBAGE IN, GARBAGE OUT

This is a technology term we use to explain erroneous conclusions coming out of a program because false data was input. The same is true for our bodies: we will get out of them what we put into them. God tells us what to eat in the Bible, and His Holy Spirit gives us wisdom for everything that is not addressed. Leviticus chapter 11 lists the clean and unclean foods. Though most people believe this is Old Testament legalism, doctors and nutritionists agree that this is much healthier eating. Though most people believe this is Old Testament legalism, doctors and nutritionists agree that this is much healthier eating. Healthier still is going back to the diet in the Garden of Eden, which consisted of seed-bearing fruits and plants (Gen. 1:29). Whatever you decide upon in your diet, be sure to partner with God in the decision-making process. He designed your body uniquely, and He knows what is best for it. Certain foods are great for some people, and not so great for others, but He can reveal specifics to you. I suggest also asking Him while you're on a fast, because your flesh will be under control, as you focus on seeking His will. Consult a nutritionist and research foods that are healthy for you also.

Food is not the only thing we put into and on our bodies. Be mindful of topical creams and antiperspirants, as they can get into your bloodstream through your pores. Research vitamins and supplements as well, because many of them have hidden ingredients, like animal fat (and worse), that you would not realize unless you researched the company.

Many of us use medications to address ailments also. While this may be necessary and helpful at times, be very careful not to overmedicate yourself. Many pharmaceutical drugs are man-made, rather than natural, and create multiple side effects, which will require more medication. Because of the greed of the pharmaceutical industry in the United States, we are one of the most medicated nations on earth. When possible, seek natural remedies for illness, and pray to God for direction when you're not sure.

Lastly, the Bible tells us not to get drunk on wine or liquor (Eph. 5:18 & Prov. 31:4-5), and in the heart of God, that includes illicit recreational drugs. Anything being ingested to alter your consciousness becomes an open door for the enemy of your soul to usurp your dominion. Remember, he is always looking for ways to do that. Don't give him an open door to your body and access to everything you hold dear—family, possessions, finances, business—because at the end of the day, God and man will hold you accountable for it.

THE TEMPLE OF THE LIVING GOD

"Don't you know that your bodies are parts of the Messiah? So, am I to take parts of the Messiah and make them parts of a prostitute? Heaven forbid! Don't you know that a man who joins himself to a prostitute becomes physically one with her? For the Tanakh [Old Testament] says, 'The two will become one flesh'; but the person who is joined to the Lord is one spirit. Run from sexual immorality! Every other sin a person commits is outside the body, but the fornicator sins against his own body. Or don't you know that your body is a temple for the Ruach HaKodesh [Holy Spirit] who lives inside you, whom you received from God? The fact is, you don't belong to yourselves; for you were bought at a price. So use your bodies to glorify God."
—*1 Corinthians 6:15-20 CJB*

God has given us many commandments in the Old and New Testaments about things we should not do with our bodies. Sexual immorality ranks highest, in that it is mentioned the most. The Lord stresses to us the dangers of sex outside of a marriage covenant between one man and one woman, because He knows the diseases and physical abuse our bodies can endure in extramarital sex and perverse sexual relationships, but it doesn't stop there. Intercourse also connects the souls of two individuals, and God does not want us connected to people and then ripped from them, connected to someone else's soul and then ripped from them, and so on.

Hence, sexual immorality attacks the health of our bodies and our souls. Instead, God wants to bless us with self-control, a fruit of the Holy Spirit (Gal. 5:22-23), and help us to find the right person with whom to make a lifelong covenant. This will bless us and propel us into our purpose, as we will now have a partner in fulfilling our goals.

God also mentions self-mutilation and tattoos (Leviticus 19:28) as activities we should abstain from when seeking to honor Him, and ourselves, with our bodies. Though these are prevalent in our culture now, they can actually lead to skin infections and diseases. Another important consideration is that we will have our bodies for the rest of our lives. Anything we put on our bodies, in the form of gashes, marks and symbols, will communicate certain things to others around us in the future. As business people, we must be aware of our appearance, to be sure it communicates wisdom, maturity and stability. Marks on one's body often communicate just the opposite.

Sure, our main topic is unlocking wealth, but we must also be mindful of the fact that God dwells within our bodies, if we invite Him. It is through each one of us that He communicates with the rest of the world. What we put in or on our bodies can either welcome God's Spirit or repel it, and we have established that His Spirit is essential for our success. Hence, honoring God with our bodies is not only healthy for us but it makes us a temple for Him to live in, thereby granting us unlimited wisdom, blessings and spiritual resources.

REST

On the 7th Day God rested from all of His work and declared that day holy. In so doing, He set a model for us of the importance of rest. He even established a weekly day of rest called the Sabbath in the 4th Commandment (Exodus 20:8-11). As a business owner, we have some flexibility in our schedules. Certain things will be non-negotiable, but much of our schedule should be set around what is best for us and what is best for our business. However, what is best for the business may sometimes conflict with what is best for you. Remember to take care of yourself and schedule weekly periods of rest.

Owning your own business can be very demanding. While most people think that business owners work fewer hours than their employees, you and I both know that business owners tend to work even harder than our employees. We are usually the first to arrive and last to leave. We're working on our businesses at home, on the road and on-site. It is very tempting to work without ceasing when you are the boss, but resist this temptation. We have already established that God has given you self-control. Now know this, He commands you to rest. Start now by building a healthy habit of scheduling "REST" in your planner for one full day each week. Success is achieved one good habit at a time. This is an essential habit if you really want the promises of God to manifest in your life. The enemy will convince you to run after money and wear yourself out. Why? Because then he can rob you when you're tired, sick or dead. The devil is a liar. God says work hard, then rest. Don't cut corners on this one. Follow the advice of your Creator. He knows what it takes for you to thrive.

SEEKING GOD FOR PHYSICAL HEALING

"In fact, it was our diseases he bore, our pains from which he suffered; yet we regarded him as punished, stricken and afflicted by God. But he was wounded because of our crimes, crushed because of our sins; the disciplining that makes us whole fell on him, and by his bruises we are healed."—Isaiah 53:4-5 CJB

Sin leads to death, and it doesn't have to be our sin. Just like a drunk driver can survive a car accident but take the life of an innocent child in the crash, so the sins of others in our nation and communities can lead us to sickness and disease. Misleading advertisements, poor business standards and greed already account for hormones, toxins and harmful additives in our food, air and water. These things alone can make us sick. If you add to that a society that is focused on working employees into early graves so that the CEOs can get richer, we have a serious health epidemic on our hands. I mention these things to you because there are times when our own choices can lead us to illness and disease, but there are other times when there are things going on around us or in our bodies of which we are not aware. But they can still kill us.

Messiah came that we might have life, and He died for our healing. So it's important that we go to God every time our bodies start to malfunction in aches, pains, illness and disease. He is willing and able to heal you. Sometimes it will be in a miraculous moment in time. Yet in most cases, God will connect you with experienced people who can help you to change your choices, so that you can help facilitate your own healing. These choices may be dietary, or they may involve rehab and exercise. Still other times they may involve surgery or medical treatment. Don't close your mind to any options until you have taken them all to God. As you seek Him in daily prayer, Bible study, worship and fasting, He will reveal His strategy for healing your body. Your job is to take the physical challenge to Him, and believe that He will respond.

Many people are unaware of this, but soul wounds can actually lead to physical illness and disease as well. Hence, God's response to you may have to do with confessing sin and asking Him to help you turn away from it. He may also tell you to be reconciled with a family member or other believer in the faith, because He knows that the resentment or offense that you carry is literally making you sick.

Resentment and offense can concentrate themselves in tissues in the body causing all types of illnesses, even cancers. For this reason, allow God to open your mind to His healing strategy as you seek Him. Then believe God for the healing. Be reminded that Messiah already bore all of our diseases and infirmities. By His wounds, we are healed. Apply the healing Blood of Messiah to every area of your body that is malfunctioning and declare God's healing daily, until it manifests.

Please note that I'm not suggesting that this is a recipe to be free of all illness forever. There may be illnesses, diseases, even physical challenges that God does not remove from you. In these cases, He is doing some other type of work, like teaching you to overcome or using you as a model of faith in the face of adversity. The reason I add this is because some believers actually accuse others of not having enough faith for healing if they aren't immediately healed. This is not always the case. Our God is a healer, and He always wants peace and wholeness for His people. Yet there are times when He will say to you, as He did to Paul, "My grace is sufficient for you, for My strength is made perfect in weakness." (2 Corinthians 12:9) At these times, you must know that God has not abandoned you or taken your illness or challenge lightly. Instead, He is planning to bless you in spite of your challenge. Trust Him at all times, and rely on His love and grace.

- KEY FIVE -
INTIMATE RELATIONSHIPS

*"**Beloved**, I pray that you may prosper in all things and be in health, just as your soul prospers."*

3 John 1:2

The final Biblical Key to unlocking wealth is intimate relationships. The word "intimate" is defined as "closely acquainted, familiar, close." Hence, as we look at intimate relationships, I am not only referring to relationships with people with whom one has intimate sexual relations, like a spouse. Instead, I'm referring to people you trust, people whose opinions you value, your inner circle. These people may be business partners and mentors, close friends and family members. In fact, the Bible suggests that we should have intimate relationships with a few key people in every area of life (Prov. 18:24 & 27:10). Yet more than that, I also suggest that you work hard at developing some level of intimacy with all of your supporters, to include your customers. When people feel connected with you, they will trust you, as long as you don't break that trust. The trust of friends, family members, business associates and clients will absolutely be key to your success as a business owner in God's Kingdom.

COACHES, TRAINERS AND MENTORS

The highlighted word in the Scripture text on the previous page, "Beloved," makes it clear that the Apostle John had an intimate relationship with those to whom he wrote this letter. It was that intimate connection that assured him that he could speak into their lives the wisdom he shares in 3rd John and that they would in fact heed his counsel. Make conscious efforts to connect with people who have been where you are going and been successful at similar endeavors. No one will be able to tell you exactly how to build your business but God. However, He will provide individuals who can set examples before you, give you wise counsel and educate you in areas that you may not have even been aware that you needed to be educated. These coaches, trainers and mentors are investing their precious time into helping you succeed. You can repay their kindness by preparing for every interaction you will have with them, and putting their suggestions into practice to create success.

When coaches, trainers and mentors make time to speak with you, be sure that you have read the books, watched the videos and researched the topics that they mentioned to you in their last interaction. Spend time also applying that which you learned from those resources to your life and business. This is how you prepare for meeting with them. It shows them that you took their counsel seriously, but it also saves precious time in your meetings with them, because they will not have to teach you fundamental principles that were in the resources they suggested for you. Instead, you can ask them questions that arose for you while availing yourself of those resources. Additionally, your preparation for meeting with them will also give you a common language during your discussion. Mentors will gladly give additional time and resources to protégés that take initiative and follow their counsel. This assures them that their time will not be wasted.

Other forms of appreciation may also be appropriate, like "thank you" cards or messages, paying for their meal at your meeting or any inexpensive item that you know they would enjoy (like a new book that is on their reading wish list). Stay away from expensive gifts and multiple gifts, as it may communicate an unhealthy attachment to your mentor. And be yourself every time you meet with them. Don't feel the need to butter them up or present yourself as someone you're not; successful people don't have time for games and they can smell ulterior motives a mile away.

CUSTOMERS, EMPLOYEES AND ASSOCIATES

As I alluded to above, you should also seek some level of intimacy with your customers, employees and associates. By this I mean that you should take interest in who they are, be genuinely concerned about them and their lives and share some details about yourself as well. This builds intimacy. Intimacy ushers us into a place in people's hearts that will influence their thoughts and decisions. When our goal is to bless them with the products and services our businesses provide, this is a great thing for our community.

As I shared earlier, people are bombarded with messages all day long. God wants them to receive His truths throughout the day as well. In fact, His Word was designed to be shared in intimate relationships, so that it would be applied easily to daily life (Deut. 6:6 & Luke 24:13-32). So often, sharing God's Word is left up to religious leaders, but in many cases, it is more effectively communicated through people we encounter on our daily journey of life. Every decision you make in your business and every word you publish is an opportunity to communicate God's Truth to those around you. Hence, you are leading, coaching and mentoring every day, in every action.

While I'm suggesting that you consciously work toward building relationships, I want to also counsel you to set healthy boundaries and enforce them. This will maintain an understanding of mutual respect between you and customers, employees and associates, allowing you to maintain your influence in their lives (Prov. 29:21). This should cause you to consider your choices more carefully and seek God for guidance and self-control throughout the day.

Take the opportunity to shine God's light into the lives of your staff, volunteers, customers and business associates every day. Your coaches and mentors should be models for you to building healthy, intimate relationships with those you serve, while maintaining healthy boundaries. You want to give God opportunities to use you in the lives of others, without giving the enemy opportunities to use others in your life. In this way, God reveals to us proper balance (Eccl. 7:16-20) and leads us to the narrow path (Matthew 7:13-14).

FAMILY RELATIONSHIPS

Family members of entrepreneurs often complain that they don't get enough time with their loved ones. With this in mind, I want to remind you that time freedom and leaving a legacy for your children's children are two important reasons for starting a business in the first place. Don't shine God's light into the lives of others and fail to be present with your family. You certainly must dedicate time to building your business, but also dedicate time to your family. Once you set times to spend with your family members, don't allow business concerns to interrupt it, if possible.

In family relationships, be sure to demonstrate the same Godly character that you exemplify in your business relationships. I have often found that believers have patience for everyone all day, but by the time they get home to their families, their patience has run out. Be sure that your family gets the best of you, not the leftovers. Failure to do so may give your spouse and children the wrong image of God's blessings and discourage them from wanting to partake in the inheritance you're establishing for them. If they see how much you enjoy running your business and that you also have the freedom to live life with them, your children and grandchildren will want to follow the model that you have set and carry on your legacy.

A practical way to carry this out is by briefly doing something peaceful and refreshing after working each day. This could be a stroll in the park, a drive through a community garden or sitting by a lake side. Whatever will give you about 20 minutes to decompress after work, so that you can walk into your house with fresh compassion for your family, plan to do that. I like to worship in my car on the way home. It allows God to minister to me and removes any negativity that would flow off of me onto my family members. If your office is at home, take a 20-minute break between working and family interactions at the end of each day. It'll have the same positive effect.

As much as possible, involve your family in your business, to the extent that they want to be involved. This will allow them to support you from a place of knowledge, and you'll get the benefit of their skills and talents. Additionally, it will communicate to your loved ones that you value them just as much as you value your business associates, which will go a long way in your family relationships.

Be sure, in all ways, that you honor your spouse and children publicly and privately, so that they will know that they take priority in your life. Bless them, while modeling the importance of hard work and commitment. As you demonstrate balance in your character and relationships with them, God's peace will fill your home, which makes operating a business so much easier and more fulfilling.

INTIMACY WITH GOD

The most important intimate relationship to your life and business must be your relationship with God Himself. The closer you get with God, the healthier your other relationships will be. God will teach you to trust and be trustworthy. He'll give you discernment of people's intentions, so that you can make decisions off of more than their words. God will heal your wounds and remove your fears so that you can truly enjoy life and business with other people, finding fulfillment and happiness along the way. As His agent in the earth, God will use you to bring more value to people's lives than you thought possible. Additionally, God will bless the relationships into which you truly invest yourself, and He will cause others to bless you through those relationships, making the people in your life valuable social and financial assets (Luke 6:38).

We began this journey looking at the intimacy God had with

the man and the woman in the Garden of Eden, just after reading about one of my encounters with the Father and Son in a vision. Hence, our journey has come full circle. Always remember that God wants to walk with you in the cool of the day every day of your life (Gen. 3:8), so invite Him into every decision and onto every excursion. Allow Him to share His heart's desires with you, while you pour your heart out to Him. These "God encounters" will undoubtedly change you in every way, transforming you into His image and likeness and propelling you into His plan for your life. Inquire of Him about the area of His vineyard that He has assigned to you, and be bold enough to ask Him for the provision and other resources needed to effectively tend it. God wants you to succeed, but before He can bless you to do so, He must share with you His definition of success. It will empower you to not only build a profitable business, but also to make a difference in the lives of people around you. That's a life well-lived. That's a life that brings glory to God and eternal rewards that will be well worth it.

MORE OPPORTUNITIES

Though this leg of our journey is coming to an end, I'd like to invest in developing an intimate relationship with you, so that together, we can create wealth to do the most good. I've placed a link below to share with you ways you can connect with me through Kingdom Wealth, LLC, and how you can receive business coaching directly from me through Prosperity Coaching™. There's a second link below to "The 7-Day Coach," a video coaching series that I would like to sow into you for FREE. "The 7-Day Coach" reveals God's Business Model established in the 7-days of creation and how to apply it to fulfill your purpose in life through building and scaling your own business. Following God's model will ALWAYS lead to success and His blessing!

The 7-Day Coach: **www.7day.coach**

Order more of these books at **www.5keysbook.com**.

Find fulfillment and success as you come to understand God's purpose for your life through our 7-week coaching program, Discovering Your Divine Design™ at **www.kingdomwealthllc.com/divine-design.**

Visit **www.kingdomwealthllc.com** for more information on ways that I can serve you and your business. Blessings!

www.ingramcontent.com/pod-product-compliance
Lightning Source LLC
Chambersburg PA
CBHW052115070526
44584CB00017B/2501